Imperfections of Beauty

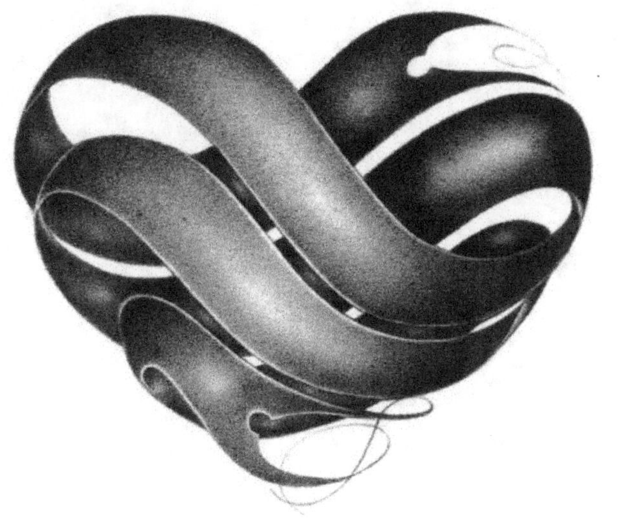

T.C. MONK

IMPERFECTIONS OF BEAUTY

T.C. MONK

Published 2022

Print ISBN: 979-8227278968

First Edition

11,293 total words

—□—

Note: All images in this book, including the cover
are hand-drawn images created by the author.

Other Works by Author

Poetry
∴

Beautiful Imperfections
(Book 2)

Sci-Fi
∴

Lumen's Quiddity
('Pariah' series)

...

Daedal Convergence
[Book 2]

...

Orphic Dénouement
[Book 3 - Due out late 2027]

Philosophy
∴

The Ties That Bind

Prison/ Nonfiction
∴

T.O.M.B.
(Those of My Blood)

Fiction
∴

Velvet Smoke

...

Beyond The Veil

Erotic
∴

Masculine Shadows

Dedication

I want to dedicate this compilation to several people I believe warrant note in my life and who have inspired some of the sentiment I've infused into this collection, even if unbeknownst to them.

To my brother Stephen, for never giving up on me, for always being there despite my less-than-appropriate actions when I was younger and during my entire incarceration. And to the rest of my family, for being there in their own way.

To Jennifer Love Hewitt, for touching the heart of a young boy and teaching him to love someone from afar, and for gracing the world with a pulchritude unrivaled by any other.

To Taylor Swift, for gifting her light to the world and sharing the essence of her lyrical sway in a way that enkindles one's soul—a truly gifted human.

To Professor Louis Mendoza for his assistance in bringing this creation to all who will read it, and for the blessing of "The Pen Project," which made this compilation possible.

To myself, for the dedication, discipline, and determination it took to create this work, for never giving up on a shattered life, and for having the will to succeed in a place where despair affects all the moments of one's beleaguered existence.

Rising from the ruins, T.C. Monk

Table of Contents

Foreword

By Louis Mendoza, Arizona State University

This is not a collection of poetry for those who are easily intimidated or want to read poetry without effort. These are not cerebral poems, but nor are they just "a spontaneous eruption of powerful feelings," or lines of rhymes as an end in itself, or a wild landscape of words and letters thrown haphazardly into the wind to land and sprout as they would, independent of one another.

The author is thoughtful. His words and images are chosen with care. They are a scaffold upon which he builds a spiritual lighthouse, a place to muse, imagine, create, conject, conjure incantations and songs, and an effort to explore and defy dimensions of time, space, and spirit. In doing so, Timothy Monk lays bare not only the shadow and light of his soul but the essential human spirit that binds us all.

Monk's poems teach us something about our shared humanity. Chiefly this, that which we love, fear, hate, and desire are inextricably and intimately related. In their relative proximity to one another, these emotional dimensions of our lives reveal our fragility, even as Monk's utterances are testimony to human resilience.

Monk is self-taught. Like flowers blooming through cracked sidewalks, his poetry is a testament to how beauty, freedom, and light can emerge from the harsh environment of containment, restraint, and unnatural shadows. In these words, assembled as poems, the reader will be provoked to think, probe one's experiences and feelings, and dive deeply in search of truths about one's own emotional journey.

Assembled over more than 20 years, these rhymes form an intellectual and emotional cartography of the author's search for emotional wisdom, truth, and peace. When one considers that Monk has been incarcerated for more than two-thirds of his life, it is difficult not to appreciate the insights offered by these poems, which are borne of a struggle to create meaning and beauty out of harsh, bleak, and sterile confinement, as well as the regret of a life constrained. Yet, one is also compelled to admire and respect the deliberate search for insight into human nature that is found in this collection.

Imperfections of Beauty is one more stone in a mountain of evidence of why we must never lose sight of the humanity of prisoners and the inhumanity of prisons. It is evidence of why efforts, large and small, to engage, support, and advance the intellectual, artistic, and emotional growth of people behind bars provide not only the authors a chance to articulate their truths, insights, and hard-earned wisdom but it is also an opportunity for redemption for those of us in the free world—if we but listen, if we but acknowledge our shared humanity and struggle for self-understanding.

Acknowledgments

I want to acknowledge the following individuals for their feedback and words of affirmation regarding my work; their feedback was invaluable and greatly appreciated. Thanks to Julie Amparano-Garcia, Rachel Jennings, Louis Mendoza, Kamala Platt, Lance Graham, and the many students enrolled in the Spring 2021 Pen Project Internship class at Arizona State University's School of Humanities, Arts, and Cultural Studies on the West Campus.

To my family, for all their support over the years, for never giving up on a lost soul, and for all their encouraging comments to "keep pushing" and "never surrender."

Imperfections of Beauty, 2018

We conjure memories into the light,
from the dark where they lay dreaming,
a sweet disorder inside the mind,
where life summons its subtle meaning.

Time is a measure of conscious thought,
a marker to expose the chaotic mind,
memories stipple its meandering path,
like scattered breadcrumbs left behind.

The boundary of morrow can never confine us
its distance is but a singular measure,
one that reveals the breadth of life,
and tests the distance of its tether.

To capture lightning in a bottle,
is but to seize a moment in time,
could it be its essence we seek,
or the unknown we wish to define?

Design in creation, reveals a purpose,
its presence fills us with solemn peace,
one proclaimed by the anvil's cry,
its Herald rising from the burning East.

Time, 2017

Life is but a skaldic measure,
an ode polished with temporal shine,
within it lies our mortal balance,
an essence lent by Father Time.

Our existence is but a mystic riddle,
a bitter pill of noetic truth,
a meter contrived by profane minds,
its colorful charade bereft of proof.

Fortune is but a fool's thread,
a measured strand to fix our wage,
the fibers of being color with season,
staining the ropes of the gallows stage.

Fame is but a grade of light,
its specious glow fades with time,
an essence tainted by foul winds,
its luster tarnished by savage minds.

Time is but an ancient melody,
a rhyme of patience we must endure,
its cadence lends a constant measure
its rhythm leaves us wanting more.

Habits of Style, 2017

Sheets of Sun to drape the skies,
a blanket of flowers to adorn the eyes.
The finery of Wind to trim the cold,
an attire of color to dress the Soul.

The wardrobe of Love to gown the day,
an ensemble of peace to clothe the way.
A sensuous garment to outfit a smile,
the regalia of Life is the vestment of style.

Cosmic Resolution, 2013

Within the bosom of the cosmos,
dwells a perfect spectrum,
its colors are so vibrant,
the world has become its reflection.

In the heart of Eternity,
abides the fire's temporal shine,
is it their essence we stem from,
the woven stardust of time?

Among the breast of Infinity,
reside creation's greatest wonders,
a world blessed with many things,
where we've become its founders.

The Troubled Heart, 2016

'Tis obscure, the streams of heart,
its quiet rage, a tempest of hope,
its bonds fragile, yet strong,
broken by fear,
a premeditated stroke.

The heart's flame, a veiled riddle
its cage, a tenuous shell,
by woven strands, the body holds,
certain madness, its touch we know.

Hatred's path, is love turned,
its quiddity, broken and alone,
hands can't hold, but surely feel,
its lonely candle, forever atone.

Born of L.O.V.E. (Links of Varied Elements), 2019

By the dust of the land,
I form the clay to hew,
with mounds of soil,
from this Earth, will I create you.

Beyond the clouds amidst the sky,
I conjure you from the blue,
by the very tempest that seethes,
out of the Wind will I weave you.

By the heat within the flame,
I will ignite something new,
a spark to emblazon the heart,
by this fire will I enkindle you.

From deepest oceans and widest seas,
I will extract what's true,
take from them the force of motion,
out of the waters will I draw you.

By the breath of existence, will I enliven you,
by the blood of being, will I imbue you,
by the gift of thought will I compel you,
by the Spirit of light will I inspire you,

and by the power of L.O.V.E....I animate you!

Things of Smiles, 2017

Tears apart from the ache of pain,
a sense of comfort within the flame.
The joys of life my thoughts of you,
birds, butterflies, and ladybugs too.
Enchanted places among the wild,
an ocean of blooms for a thousand miles.
A subtle whisper, a sultry grin,
a fear that vanishes from within.
Snowflakes descending from the sky,
moments of brilliance that make us shine.
The heart we give, the breath we breathe,
are 'Things of Smiles' we all need.

Interest hidden beneath the surface,
promises made with meaningful purpose.
A soft embrace, a lover's sigh,
hope gift wrapped in a child's eyes.
Moments we wish would last forever,
pleasures we create when we're together.
The dreams we live, the gift of time,
the grace of life, a love that binds.
A fluorescent sunset to capture the eye,
the Moon at night to reveal the tide.
The Sun, the Sky, the morning dew,
these 'Things of Smiles' bless me and you.

Sensual whispers, those meant to please.
delicate kisses that weaken the knees.
The Stars, the Moon, Fireflies at night,
little things to bring our eyes to life.
A smile that warms, a touch that heals,
the shared secrets only lovers reveal.
Dandelions, murmurs, blown kisses of care,
things that move delicately upon the air.
A hand to hold, a love of worth,
grace that exists beyond this Earth.
Simple things, a friend that's true,
these 'Things of Smiles' comfort our blues.

Enormous waterfalls and babbling brooks,
fantasies we live inside of books.
Puppy dog eyes, and kitten paws,
wondrous things that give us pause.
Gentle lips upon a lover's eyes,
the truth of love we cannot hide.
Majestic fields of green reds and gold,
purples, blues, and ambers that glow.
The motley flowers, the soothing shade,
blossoms we drop along the way.
A message that reveals the final clue,
how 'Things of Smiles' are made for two.

Things of Tears, 2017

Pain born of breathless laughter,
aches appearing for days after.
The loss of time, promises broken,
unforgettable love, words unspoken.
Passion unchained, sunlight rays,
feelings of regret, the sound of blame.
Butterfly kisses, shame that's hidden,
sympathetic eyes, sins unforgiven.
The touch of loneliness, being worlds apart,
unshared scars strangling the heart.
Songs of hope, words of pain,
these 'Things of Tears' we all feel the same.

Winning the race, coming in last,
meaningful kisses, losing one's past.
Puppy dog yelps, and kitten claws,
reliving the agony of things we saw.
Trust that's broken, faith that's lost,
the balance remaining after paying the cost.
Stolen hearts, regretful lives,
shame and sorrow, the things we hide.
Terror unchecked, betrayals that last,
lives that vanish much too fast.
A river of lies, a treachery of greed,
are 'Things of Tears' that make us bleed.

Deceit that dwells behind gentle eyes,
frauds that speak truths that lie.
Haunted dreams, things of fear,
a precious smile no longer here.
A memory, a thought, things we feel,
the message they bring, leave scars unhealed,
The needle, the drugs, the death we seek,
the specious pleasures that make us weak.
Emotions that burn, loves that fade,
sentimental attachments that vanish in flames.
Precious moments, the gift of life,
are 'Things of Tears' that cut like a knife.

Salt in the wound, shade that burns,
scars unveiled, feelings that spurn.
Touched by an angel, the prick of a thorn,
dreams unspoken, hope that's scorned.
Missions of need, believing what you learn,
realizing you're a saint spreading the devil's word.
Hearts that change, hopes that blind,
false forgiveness, faiths that lie.
A life cut short, a heaven much nearer,
details of the truth multiply in the mirror.
Forbidden fruits, the dangers they hide,
are 'Things of Tears' that break us inside.

Things of Hope, 2017

Safety beyond a sense of need,
love cultivated from the tiniest seed.
Beauty that moves us from afar,
the gift of light from a distant star.
Anger that fades by gentlest touch,
forgiveness offered without a crutch.
A sense of grace within the dark,
the absence of fear within the heart.
A genuine smile that imparts care,
love enjoyed without judgment or fear.
Inspiring thoughts, deeds of valor,
weave 'Things of Hope' in our most desperate hour.

Feelings of joy, the touch of pride,
shared laughter we cannot hide.
Wishful eyes, the want of more,
the needs of desire that stoke our core.
Love returned once its lent,
life renewed upon prayers of sentiment.
The gift of freedom, a promise to protect,
hymns we fashion into prayers that bless.
The fight for life, peace, and liberty,
the pursuit of happiness, love, and longevity.
The hand of trust, the promise of redemption,
weave 'Things of Hope' to comfort our apprehension.

A warmth that enkindles without touch,
a diamond that sparkles from every cut.
A reassuring feeling when no one's around,
a voice of comfort bereft of sound.
The sense of strength from somewhere deep,
dreams that manifest among the world of sleep.
The color of music, the song of light,
an essence that bestows the bounty of life.
The blending of souls, a life that's new,
plaited by the threads of destiny's loom.
Dreams of tomorrow, the blessings we speak,
weave 'Things of Hope' we all seek.

Times we share, the comfort of memory,
the eyes of a child in constant reverie.
The essence of Sun, the shine of Moon,
infusing our lives with things that renew.
A mystery solved, a meaningful lesson,
a reliance of faith, belief beyond question.
The charm of making, an enchanted melody,
tears of comfort, ones born of threnody.
A memory that heals, a wrong that's righted,
the power of forgiveness once recited.
Honor, trust, compassion that's true,
these 'Things of Hope' are born for two.

Things of Fear, 2017

The torment of loss beyond consolation,
forbidden nectars that corrupt preservation.
Thoughts of madness, evils untold,
demented actions, the loss of control.
The resident evil that dwells within,
depravity hidden behind a charming grin.
The absence of hope, the depth of greed,
manifest the horrors that abide in dreams.
The fever of lunacy, gods of hate,
the chant of demons delivered by saints.
The beast of terror, a sinister host,
these 'Things of Fear' we dread the most.

A deity that fails, the blessing of sins,
perfidy disguised as holy doctrine.
The path of uncertainty, the tether's end,
courage that fails in the lion's den.
A hand that grasps us from the deep,
the fiends that ravage us in our sleep.
The eyes of wickedness, heaven's wrath,
the promise of salvation in God's laugh.
The winds of change, the unseen storm,
the agony and pain of a child stillborn.
A trust that's lost, a well run dry,
from these 'Things of Fear' we cannot hide.

Dangers that dwell among the unseen,
calamity that brings us to our knees.
Tears of blood, a cure that robs,
an angel of hell, a halo of barbs.
Truths that lie, smiles that kill,
the charade of false evidence appearing real.
A specious faith, a savior of doom,
a primrose path from cradle to tomb.
Amnesty lost, revenge that turns,
souls that bathe in a lake that burns.
The skin of evil, creation unmade,
these 'Things of Fear' will never fade.

Flowers that weep, trees that scream,
the tonic of wickedness from Eden's stream.
Icy waters that steal your breath,
those who are baptized in the lake of death.
An elixir of misery, a brew of greed,
nectars that nourish the enemy's seed.
Sins that heal, blessings that burn,
a curse you weave from prayers you learn.
A presence you feel, a deceptive touch,
the hands that defile are wrought from trust.
Belief becomes the currency of trade,
these 'Things of Fear' are human made.

Reverie, 2013

Immeasurable agony paints my mind,
its harrowing color is my torment,
the waves of misery assailing me,
are sufferances of my own invent.

My sleeping echoes mask the verity,
of the senseless nothing I've become,
I pray thee for an ever slumber,
immerse my heart beneath something numb.

The Greatest Sin, 2002

I prayed alone for a long time,
I prayed alone for some kind of sign,
I prayed for them to see and know,
I prayed for them to let you go.

I heard the evil these men would do,
I heard the lies they did spew,
I heard them cry, 'deceit and fraud',
I heard them curse the Son of God.

I felt the whip and every lace,
I felt the pain upon your face,
I felt the thorns upon your head,
I felt the blood that you have shed.

I wept aloud as I saw your face,
I wept aloud for their disgrace,
I wept aloud, up to the sky,
I wept aloud, 'Why, Father, Why?'

I saw the place where you were led,
I saw the ground where you had bled,
I saw the cross to which you'd been tied,
I saw the hill where you had died.

I know it was for me you cared,
I know it was My cross you bared,
I know it was your greatest sign,
I know it was for all mankind.

I knelt and prayed with all my breath,
I knelt beside your place of rest,
I knelt to heaven and made this plea,
I knelt and cried, 'My God, forgive me!'

I kept my faith from that time,
I kept your memory in my mind,
I kept to all that I have learned,
I kept a constant vigil for your return.

Impressions, 2019

Beyond the veil of arcanum,
resides the knowledge we all seek,
hidden here be charms of making,
with creation's voice dare we speak.

'Tis a riddle that must be solved,
a mystic code to reveal the rhyme,
an ancient script once it's spoken,
quickly vanishes from the mind.

Within the glass of hour's age,
exists the measure we all seek,
by the grains of sand there do fall,
reckon the moments of life we keep.

Upon destiny's most sacred loom,
are woven the threads of time,
and by the hands of cogent fate,
are we grafted onto the vine.

The Sleep, 2019

The pains of life drift away,
in the warmth of distant sleep,
like the vanishing of the gloam,
beyond the horizon of the deep.

It is here among the silence,
we give license to our dreams,
and draw forth fallow thoughts,
from beneath its specious stream.

Beyond the veil of vigilance,
exist the vagaries of our slumber,
a measure to mete the scales
a tether to keep us under.

Behind the quate we should listen,
as beauty weaves its calm repose,
in the silent depth we proffer,
copper wishes to knit our souls.

As our respite begins to vanish,
and the visions start to wane,
let the dawn rouse our minds,
from the fertile fields of play.

Shades of Light, 2016

Night enfolds the distant stars,
like raw diamonds wrapped in coal,
their subtle light imbues the deep,
where the eyes of creation glow.

Threads of amber cast a halo,
around the fires of the night,
embers burn against the dark,
like wildflowers born of light.

Flames that shine beyond the veil,
create the shadows ring,
a tether woven by the night,
to trammel a savage thing.

Rose and Lament, 2014

By her touch we are smitten,
in a place where all love grows,
by her grace we are humbled,
in the light her beauty is known.

'Tis the rose we all love,
the tender core within its folds,
its vivid color hastens the blood,
and often warms the coldest soul.

The day be graced by her scent,
amid a field of wildflowers,
her beauty is love and lament,
eternity's glass shades her power.

Reflections of Xanadu, 2007

Relaxing beneath a liquid sky, I watched as pregnant
clouds slipped behind the lime-green fronds of a crooked
palm, which seemed to grow from the very cinnamon-colored
sand of the beach, next to my harlequin fanback chair.

I bathed beneath the daystar as it journeyed across
the turquoise empyrean, asking little in return, merely
wishing to spread its essence upon the petals of every
flower, to brighten the layers of every cloud, to bleed
upon every blade of grass, to stroll across the dry desert,
and to see its own reflection in a curtain of rain.

I felt the Sun warming my flesh, and enjoyed the scent
of its bouquet, as it lingered upon my skin, fresh and
redolent like the sweet smell of warm honey flowing
from the comb. Its narcotizing fragrance held me captive
until I felt its quintessence fade away, hiding itself behind a
windsurfing cloud, and leaving me with a butternut nevus.

I reached out and touched the caller wind, and it touched me
back tenderly. It wrapped its essence about me, like a
formfitting coat, and held me as though I were its lover. I stole
a deep inhalation, and even though the zephyr was no longer
present I could still smell the Sun's ambrosial scent, where
it had nuzzled against me, as if I were a wildflower.

Thick beads of condensation raced down my glass,
as fat cubes of ice, like raw diamonds,
cooled my coffin varnish, cracking themselves open,
and clinking against the glass.

Tawny-colored age stones rose from the foundations of the world, like giant jagged blades that cut sharply across the welkin, biting deep into the horizon, as if trying to swallow the firmament whole with its infinite maw.

A niveous lace caressed the beach from the sapphire sea creating a necklace of white foam encircling the strand. Out among the empire of blue were what looked like myriad tiny jewels, sparkling like flash bulbs, where each wave seemed to capture thousands of watery photographs of the gulls swirling above, the crystal rain as it fell, and the Sun, where it lay natant in the aether like a giant eye, ever-watchful.

It even seemed to capture flicks of the infinite universe, and maybe of the Creator too, where it omnipotently moved through the cosmos casting worlds among the stars.

Maybe the waves even took pictures if me, sitting on a caramel sandy beach, next to a snake-like palm tree, on a particolored throne, beneath a generous sky, with fertile woolpacks, and a lemon-yellow Sun.

Elements of Life, 2016

Within the eye rests the storm,
upon the fringes abides its charm,
is it the calm that wields its might,
or the threshold which does us harm?

Behind the flame lies the spark,
an ethereal offering to bring us hope,
is it fervent to conceal its secret,
or candent to help us cope?

Beneath the waves dwells a stillness,
a gifted element to nourish the land,
a quiddity that has no equal,
an essence to humble the toughest man.

Among the world resides all things,
even the light to bathe the shade,
for nothing is hidden among this land,
not even the path to our own grave.

Beyond this world exists the unknown,
where the spirit travels when it leaves,
it carries the blessings we all speak,
and the prayers of love we weave.

Remembrance, 2012

We commend our dead beneath the earth,
to the flames, the deep, to our place of birth,
it is for their return, we pray in vain,
a sorrow that cripples us with immeasurable pain.

Our endless tears are unable to quench,
the unbearable silence exposed by their absence,
what strangles our thoughts with woeful regret,
are the words and things we've not shared yet.

We summon their image like a flame from the dark,
a warmth we embrace to console the heart,
it's their presence we miss, the solace we shared,
of those we've loved, and for those we've dared.

A thought, a scent, stimulates the mind,
subtle moments of them, captured in time,
their memories comfort us, with their love of life,
such remnants warm us, with the hope of light.

These were our lovers, our life-long friends,
those we cared for, and for those we defend,
it is their spirit we remember, their comfort and kiss,
a playmate, a companion, we dearly miss.

I Pine, 2011

I lust to burn with passion's pyre,
I hope to drown in love's attire,
I long to dream in cosmic color,
I endeavor to find my eternal lover.

I hunger to feed on death's desire,
I seek to consume the heart of sapphire,
I thirst to taste the waters of glory,
I hunt to feast on Nature's quarry.

I crave to know the secret of fire,
I pray to learn the Angel's lyre,
I yearn to speak the immortal rhyme,
I wish to solve the riddle of Time.

I breathe to inherit the gift to inspire,
I strive to collect the things I admire,
I choose to pursue the undying light,
I bathe to assume the fragrance of life.

Chronon, 2020

The measure of age is a grain of sand,
its sum is finite within the glass,
the temporal gauge inside its crown,
is a portion shared between its halves.

Its tawny treasure holds infinite value,
a degree of existence we've come to know,
as Eternity's essence begins to vanish,
fragments of Time begin to grow.

A Message to Ruminate, 2007

I wonder if the world can fathom the primrose
path that has extinguished the candle of my life.
How the polychrome of life's kaleidoscope,
paints the canvas of my future to be,
and the remaining gamut of trials
I am yet to suffer beneath the scourge.

My essence is barren, save for the memories haunting
the quietude (of the tempest), hiding among the many
warrens of the chaotic labyrinth that is the hollow
dungeon of my mind. I am the empty reflection
trapped at the edges of the glass, swimming in a
maelstrom of talons, which rives all my hopes, and
drowns them in a deluge of despair.

I feel the bonfire hemorrhaging from the heart of darkness,
spilling liquid shadows upon my soul, to feed on the raw sea of
perfidy that flows within my veins, from perdition's own cauldron.

Do you think the world could surmise the genesis of
emotion's first impulse, or the site of its maiden strike,
as the heart cheats the will of freedom?

I wonder if they can fathom the chains that continually
strain against the barriers of my sanity. Or how the madness
that lies beneath this façade of calm I struggle to control
perpetually, is but a storm that awaits behind an empty wall
of silence, hiding the myriad nightmares that have masked
themselves in a cloak of many colors, concealed among
a mirage of blissful dreams.

Would they even understand the fragments of shattered glass
that separate the pieces of my life in the mirror of deception?
Could they even comprehend the montage of images among
the slivers? Or the picture puzzle of a thousand dreams draining
from my memory like the sand through the hourglass of age?

The world may never know the trials of my soul,
or how it breathes the sulfur, masked as the smoke of hope,
or taste deception's echoes lacing the empty promises of
those who feed on the credulity of others.

Such things are veiled
in camouflage and simply reflect the shades of righteousness,
those forged in the milieu of illusion.

Dreams, 2006

I hear the wind chimes in the distance,
as they echo across my soul,
their melodies are the night songs,
telling tales of ages old.

These songs are but mystic riddles,
of days that have come before,
of things that once were
and of a peace that is no more.

How can the dreams of tomorrow,
be our saviour from the cold,
when they vanish much too quickly,
like the warmth of an old soul.

The past lay behind me,
like footprints in the sand,
shattered remnants of my life,
reflected in the broken glass.

There is a melody in the distance,
which sings the myths of old,
these paeans are the wind songs,
the Minstrel's voice to caress my soul.

These ballads are of ancient fables,
of things that are no more,
of a time when we once were,
and of lives that came before.

I hear the solemn laughter,
echoing like a distant scream,
raging through my troubled mind,
smiting the beauty within my dreams.

I hear the wailings in the night,
their clarion, a solemn cue,
the remnants that still echo,
foretell the death of my Muse.

Symmetry, 2002

The dark constricts to smother the light,
its sinister shadow ministers the night
Its baleful essence chills the heart,
the light endures to appease the dark.

Death was born to extinguish life,
a thing of fear to invent strife.
It condemns our bodies to immortal rest.
life was woven to inspire death.

Vice was bred to corrupt our virtue,
to defile the body with delights we value.
Pain and pleasure are the whips that entice,
virtue is the cradle to pamper vice.

The sinner blossoms to groom the saint,
and imbues its apprentice with insidious taint.
It bestows its counsel upon the beginner,
until the saint wilts and becomes a sinner.

Fear abides in the smoke of hope,
its delicate ribbons weave a rope.
The gallows reflect in fortune's mirror,
hope exists to expose our fear.

Sun doth smother the glorious shade,
it condemns the silhouette to an early grave.
Shade now strangles its heavenly splendor,
the tomb frees the banished specter.

Love fashions the ties of hate,
it breaks the bonds we strive to create.
Enmity shatters the chains of passion,
yet toils and shapes the fantasies we imagine.

Courage suffocates the spirit of doubt,
it poisons the waters of Nature's fount.
Dubiety stifles the heart of the bold,
the well of valor forges the soul.

Chance stirs the wheel of fate,
it dooms the path we choose to take.
Destiny binds the wings of favor,
desire shares the fortune we savor.

Trust paves the road to betrayal,
it damns the myth within the fable.
Perfidy is a blessing disguised as faith,
the legend endures with belief in grace.

The Second Hunt, 2004

Beneath the shroud of Winter's mane,
lies the beast within its den,
an enchanted slumber holds its sway,
as dreams of its 2nd hunt begin.

The scent of prey blankets the field
like the fragrance of morning rose,
helping the predator stalk its quarry,
and chase it to and fro.

With tooth and claw painted red,
and its feral craving sated,
it cleans its muzzle with its paw,
of the mess its savagery created.

With its hunger aptly appeased,
and belly plump with fine cuisine,
it allows its mind to be at rest,
till it wakes by warmth of Spring.

A Relic of Theorem, 2006

Raging malice beneath an empty calm,
brings sinister purpose that fades to black,
with a spellbinding ring of cold betrayal,
lies the message within the hollow glass.

In facing death we become alive,
a bitter pill of human grace,
within the mirror bleeds our corruption,
and sings the paean of future's fate.

We bleed in vain with quiet solace,
endure the past with wailing silence,
embrace the fangs of placid havoc,
with drops of malice to nourish the heart.

Feeding life to an empty grave,
moving silence against the seam,
where madness gains the final laugh,
and faith grows against the grain.

Fueling fire with empty words,
communing with shadows among the flames,
reciting the phrases upon the wall,
each one a passion that slowly fades.

Underworld reality corrupts my patience,
freeing blessings in a lonely whisper,
on a stage laced with barren candles,
each one a story that ends in pain.

A Museful Quiddity, 2002

Empty silence belies my wisdom,
akin to a tempest beyond perception,
ill begotten by dreams I have lived,
muffled by echoes that hold no sway.

Beyond the certain exists the unknown,
trapped by the fear of uncertain change,
held in thrall by false proclamations,
wishing to exist for more than servitude.

Time is amorphous, like ordered chaos,
an evanescent brume to shroud our existence,
a collective ruin of what is forgotten,
are mere reflections of our own mortality.

The truth of life is masked by dreams,
fleeting and ephemeral like vanishing smoke,
and within the eyes of a condemned soul,
I glimpsed life unshaded, undisguised.

Tainted knowledge has scorched my life,
like charred ruins upon the hearth,
held interred until I return,
unbeknownst in the breast of ash.

Within the flame doth march Time's riddle,
imparting the illusion of inscrutable secrets,
my world is but a mirage before me,
denying the promise of true Nirvana.

A Perfect Illusion, 2003

We live within a wakeless dream,
woven by the shades of life,
pouring forth from the dark abyss,
reflections within the mirror black.

Breaking the pane to erase reality,
in vain we shatter the face of madness,
to escape the master of truth's illusion
where splintered shards pave the stage.

Dark is the mind of absent reason,
a malicious banquet on which we feast,
a chalice filled with self-deception,
a table set with specious grandeur.

We are but captives of pretentious indifference,
a prison to which we are manner born,
trapped by the vanity of reputation,
held interred by the web of impudence.

All vengeance is an empty halo,
a crown laden with morbid reason,
worn on the brow of constant misery,
an illusion fraught with intrepid sentiment.

Divergence, 1999

Life——that fading candle among the dark,
how it sways with the wind's gentle melody,
it paints the night with frolicking shadows,
the promise of hope lies in its mystery.

Death——that sacred fire which consumes us all,
oh, how soft be its invisible touch,
harsh be the season that buries our love,
in the stars are written the story of us.

Immortality——that elusive charm we all seek,
a boon that hides behind our strife,
a gift that lies between humble death,
and this nightmare we call...life.

Sailing Eternally, 2005

My voyage began at the break of dawn,
upon the surface of the sun-jeweled sea,
I felt the salt-spray touch my face,
and watched the sails billowing in the breeze.

As I gazed across the empire of blue,
at a mirage the doldrums spun,
I marveled at the grand illusion,
where the sky and ocean became one.

As I crossed the highway of the sea,
I saw not the danger it belied,
no portent of the coming storm,
only the specious quietude of tide.

A sudden darkness filled the air,
as I sailed into the caller wind,
waiting for the horizon to change,
for the invisible tempest to begin.

A baleful wind began to whisper,
of chilling things I was soon to know,
the noshing of teeth upon my flesh,
the stropping of claws upon my bones.

I then looked upon the heart of darkness,
swimming around me in the frigid depths,
waiting beneath the empty calm,
were its icy fangs of death.

It was then I heard a haunting ballad,
the allure of a Siren's melody,
it was a rhyme to lure this ancient mariner,
to his sepulcher beneath the sea.

I crashed upon the jutting rocks,
another victim for the ocean's grave,
to forever roam the darkness,
a silent prisoner beneath the waves.

Now I sail the eternal sea,
beneath rolling waves of liquid glass,
on an armada filled with immortal salts,
those fallen heroes of the past.

Built to Shine, 2006

{Part 1}

Straight from the pit where the devil dwells,
I was woven from the flames in the bowels of hell,
to spread like a plague among mortal man,
to smash all the dreams that paradise planned.

There is no escape from the evil that creeps,
on the land, in the sea, among the world of sleep,
wicked thoughts we create within our dreams,
breeds hate that pervades like a savage scream.

My blood is the fuel that feeds the flames,
driving the essence of my violent campaigns,
from the cosmos I was woven by the hands of time,
from the heart of a star, I was built to shine.

Legions of the Damned, 2002

I've always been told I was spawned from hell,
that beneath my facade there's a demon who dwells,
that I'm part of the jetsam, lost wreckage in the sand,
they say I've been forsaken, to the legions of the damned.

In my trials of life, I've wondered many things,
but found only questions... without essence or meaning.
I can show you many things, take you to the promise land,
a place of many wonders you may never understand,
a world of many evils, just beyond the night,
where your mind is overwhelmed by the profusion of sight.

I'm adrift in the darkness on an endless tether,
All alone in the void, among the aether forever,
and here's where you'll know that breath was your last,
when the devil reaches out through the cracks in the glass.
Even to the roots you're a dedicated fan,
one of the elites of the legions of the damned.

I come from a place where no one's ever been,
a stranger from the deep, an elemental of wind.
I've held counsel on the rings of many worlds afar,
spreading my message among the people of the stars.
Reasons we craft are a means to an end,
to justify the actions of a necessary sin.

Doomsday weapons are currently the craze,
rendering nations to ashes with their enigmatic blaze.
Cold is the world and its wicked little ways,
truth is the message; the evidence is shame.
I wonder if they'll ever... truly understand,
what it means to pledge allegiance,
to the legions of the dammed.

It's true I've been oppressed for most of my life,
kept under guard, bereft of any rights.
They say I'm the last of an evil breed,
to be stamped out like one of Satan's seeds.
I saw the truth from their own hand,
they sentenced me to death, as the gavel hit the stand.

Though I spoke my peace, expressed my point of view,
they took me to the gallows, and that's when I knew,
this fate was real, it was the end of the line,
death was upon me... but it wasn't my time.
And because I never lost faith in the who I am,
this is how I joined the legions of the damned.

Now here's a message, for those not in the grave,
expression is the truth, and freedom is the way.
So, rise to your feet and make your stand,
be a beacon of light, write your message in the sand.
Be true to the reasons and the wars you wage,
patience is the sand in the hourglass of age.

The essence of the world is trapped in your brain,
remember, freedom is the life bereft of the chains.
So, travel the world, and express your mind,
the only thing that's free, is the passage of time.
I thought I knew how to let my wings unfurl,
I guess I was wrong, now I'm chained in this world.

So, keep in mind when it all goes insane,
heed this message if you need help in the game,
call me from beyond, if there's no other plan,
I'll rise from the ashes and bring the legions of the damned.

What Awaits, 2003

Now I find myself drifting through the cosmic stream,
as I slip into the nether world of undreamt dreams.
Falling down a spiral, destination unknown,
a maelstrom of violence steady tearing at my soul.
As I pass through the veil I hear a solemn chant,
coming from the faces in the flames of the lamp.
It's their pain and rage reaching out from the grave,
in the blink of an eye I knew I was to blame.
And like ghosts from the past with an evil need,
they wove rings from the smoke into chains to bind me.

Through the flames of their world, I saw the spectrum change,
glimmers of my life, past pleasures, and pain.
Like bolts of lightning, they ravaged my mind,
coursing through my head, leaving madness behind.
I'm still not sure if I truly know,
where my bones will rest, or my essence will go.
But from what I've seen, and where I've been,
it won't be at the place where the rainbow ends.
I'm a firm believer in, "... reap what you sow",
and we pay those dues at the end of the road.

As I pass the next level and go beyond,
the pain increases and the memories are strong.
I feel so out of place, so haunted by my fears,
this primrose path, is my trail of tears,
a place of many sorrows, with lessons to learn,
a lifetime of madness among the flames that churn.
It was here that I fell, and the demon smoked,
the last of my essence, and I hoped he choked.
Now I know... it was the Fates who sold,
the remains of my life, and the dust of my bones.

I claw back to the top of this dreadful tier,
and pray for an end to this relentless nightmare.
Once I am free from this wicked dream,
I hope I never hear another soulless scream.
From the emptiness beyond I hope I never need,
to cross into the depth where the darkness bleeds.
for those who try to really tempt fate,
there is a penance before you pass through the gate.
As I look into the mirror, I find the emptiness cold,
reaching out is a hand to collect what's owed.

Once again, I'm inside the world that I dread,
plagued by the sorrows and the screams of the dead.
The faces in the flames are all still there,
raping my mind and exploiting my fears.
Even in my dreams their world seems real,
and when I'm awake, it's their madness I feel.
I scream at the nightmares, and hope they pass,
trapped in the mirror at the edges of the glass.
I'm forced to seek shelter... on the inside,
but there's no place to go, no refuge to hide.

The evil that pervades from within this place,
is wrought from the clay of my own disgrace.
But now I truly see... with my own eyes,
the horrors that await me, on the day that I die.

Profundity[1], 2019

I am incapable of discerning the form of you,
yet your wondrous essence inspires me to.
Your embrace clings to me like a fleece,
an ineffable element of fear and peace.

Upon your skin your strength is wild,
beneath, you cradle me, like a child.
Your limpid nature moves like the wind,
and chills the bones beneath my skin.

Absent a road, you forge a path,
your substance sculpts the rocks like glass.
Within heaven's mirror we see our author,
the essence defining the shape of water.

Love Cuts, 2019

Beneath love dwells a simple silence,
like the calm before a storm,
it gives license to our fears
and imbues our thoughts with form.

In love we place a mighty trust,
a faith we believe is more than real,
we pray for it to comfort us
and banish the doubts we feel.

When love sings, we all should listen
to the rhyme of its fervent meaning,
its precious rhythm brings us reason
and silent hope to our being.

About love we vividly ponder
all the colors of this life,
we marvel at its complexity
and bathe happily in its light.

Within love resides a quiet grace
one of profound belief,
a gift greater than any freedom
and as strong as any peace.

By divine love we all live
in a state of chaotic bliss,
an ever-changing kaleidoscope
bringing balance to all we cherish.

All love is but counted sand
in the glass of Time's trust,
its essence vanishes like the rain,
through the channel that love cuts.

Elementals, 2004

The night watches with a thousand eyes
I wonder if they know of what I dream,
is it they who collect my penny wishes,
or the sprites who live in the stream?

The forest is vibrant with a million cries
I wonder if they can feel my pain,
do they know the rhythm to charm the seasons
or the rhyme to enchant the rain?

The wind is fraught with a billion sighs
I wonder from whence it truly came,
its nature enkindles my humble spirit
and nourishes the heart within the flame.

The sea is teeming with a trillion lives
I wonder if they know what I am,
or how I wish to return to them
to swim free in the ocean again.

Timeless Pain, 2003

All my life I've searched for better ways
to escape the madness and these traces of gray.
From the bottom of the world I watch the April rain,
travel down my window like wax from a flame.

So much time has now gone by,
was it really worth it, I often wonder why.
It's a painful lesson for anyone to learn,
like the flame at the tip of a candle that burns.

Everything I view seems so surreal,
a dreamlike illusion in this dungeon of steel.
Traces of those who've come before,
markin' this cage, the walls and the door.
A frantic message carved in the blocks,
those poetic words read "Will it EVER stop?"

These walls that hold me, they know my pain,
there's a message in the rocks, and a song in the chains.
A rhyme for the season, a rhythm to the rain,
it's a winsome song of which remains the same.

Most of my life I just sat still,
waiting for things to come as they will,
always hoping for more from my solemn life,
I've got three walls and a door holding me tight!

I struggle each day with the passage of time,
my prayers go unanswered even when they shine,
I never lose faith, it's what keeps me SANE,
even when I miss all the seasons that change.

Rhymes are the jewels we string like pearls,
rhythm is the motion that moves the world.
My destiny is about me, it falls like the rain,
the Fates owe me dues and some change.

I hold my faith and conquer my ground,
patience is a virtue, and the silence is loud.
A somber message fills these ocean eyes,
tell me, do you see the wretched demon they hide?

Behind this sea of pain, the windows to the soul,
deep down inside, how much do they show?
Trapped in my mind the memories are haunting,
remember the look of a dead man walking.

Every day I trudge the same old path,
leaving dust in my wake with every minute of sand.
For the final account in damnations game,
it's the nameless graves where our innocence lay.

There will be a time to rest when I reach the grave.
When my ghost is gone, will they still know my name?

My Friend, 2018

An adversary haunted me most of my life,
its essence created doubts in my mind,
It kept me down and smothered my trust,
and almost ruined everything I touched.

I had lost my faith in most of humanity,
my patience was stretched to the edge of insanity,
But then one day I met a very sage man,
who changed my thoughts and how I stand.

It was here I learned how the words I lend,
won me the love and respect of my friend,
Loneliness is a hard road we solemnly tread,
but it's filled with the sustenance of our daily bread.

If it were not for these gems we haply find,
life would be dull, bereft of their shine.
I am grateful to have met one of the best,
it must have taken amazing grace...
and all of heaven's breath.

I am careful now with the days I spend,
as each new morning...is a gift from my friend.

No Tomorrow, 2007

I feel the drums, the rumble,
with a thunderous sound,
I feel the rhythm, the motion,
as they shake the ground.

I know my words, my rhymes,
they share this paean,
it's the only way my heart
can express my pain.

I hear the cymbals, they crash,
and ring in my ear,
as the sticks bounce back
and the music appears.

I touch the mic, it breathes,
a solemn chant,
the dreams of tomorrow
are illusions in the lamp.

I see the music, it moves,
like smoke on the glass,
floating' in the aether,
dissipating too fast.

I taste the gold, the fame,
and all the prestige,
it's for the love I receive
why I continue to breathe.

I mean the words, the depth,
in the lyrics I phrase,
they're reflections of my mind,
expressions of my strain.

There's no tomorrow, today,
the future's unknown,
I use it like money
I've had too long.

I spend it too fast
everywhere I go,
yesterday's gone,
there is no tomorrow.

I show the faith, the discipline,
in all that I do,
it's a life I've created
out of scraps that are used.

I want the most, the best,
of all that is real,
a Muse in my life
to inspire my will.

I cannot run, escape,
this life of mine,
the things I will do
will resound across time.

I only wish, desire,
for the world to see,
all the beautiful things
my mind can weave.

I can trust, honor,
the words from the past,
they ring true with a message
not to live too fast.

I can accept, embrace,
there will come a time,
when the wind doesn't blow,
and the Sun don't shine.

I can't imagine, believe,
these times are my last,
I'll surely miss the world
and all that it has.

It's all gone now,
except for the sorrow,
I better live now,
cause there is no tomorrow!

Alone, 2001

I remember, when you were here,
it was long ago, once upon a year.
It was today, I felt the pain,
the tears on my shoulder, felt like the rain.

Now I'm sitting alone watching the clock,
I feel the strains of another tear drop.
Ticking the hours watching them change,
counting the days, that you've been away.

I try to be strong in all that I do,
but nothing else matters, when it comes to you.
You tell me in letters everything'll be fine,
you're watching over me, in every sunrise.

You made me laugh and often smile,
sometimes your letters made me sad for a while.
I remember your promise to sing with the dawn,
and the light would be our little love song.

Now I rise every day while it's still night,
so, I don't miss your psalm in every twilight.
You told me one day, when I'd seen turtledoves,
perched on my window they were sent with your love.

You said they were gifts while we're apart,
in each one you wrapped a little piece of your heart.
I cannot express how bad I need you here,
my life is incomplete when you're not near.

So, until the day when you come home,
your love is my comfort when I'm ... Alone.

Sunshine, 1994

Sometimes it's a dream and nothing seems real,
even when I try there's nothing left to feel.
The vanishing memories, of days gone past,
there's nothing else left, not even my laugh.
Try as I may, to remember the time,
when they locked out the wind and stole the sunshine.

Every day seems the same, I need something new,
to help ease the pain of this morbid view.
Out in the field beyond my window,
I see the boughs sway as the wind blows.
Down comes the rain, fogging up the glass,
obscuring the view, of mother nature's wrath.
Even to this day I continue to try,
to hear the song of the rain and feel the sunshine.

Locked away here in this concrete grave,
it's the little things I miss and the pleasures I crave.
The only thing that's hard is keeping hope alive,
as the walls close in trying to shatter my mind.
A mental trap, one to break me down,
the screams in my mind are the only sane sounds.
Just one time before I die,
I want to see the moonrise in the sunshine.

Some days I dream of things I feel,
when I really try sometimes it seems real.
The memories I have fall like sand in the glass,
they fade away slowly as the years drift past.
Sometimes I wish that one day soon,
I could meet the man who lives in the Moon.
I'd ask him why he doesn't come down,
and kick it on my window when there's no one around,
to talk about things, reminisce old times,
chat about the weather, reflect the sunshine.

The days become one as time goes by,
trapped in this cage, merely waiting to die.
Lucky are those who have a second chance,
to live once more among the common mass,
instead of trapped inside where the days are marked,
where walls whisper your name and demons rule the dark.
I know it's true and its hard time,
when the walls block out, all the sunshine.

I know right now, where I'd rather be,
on the outside, being wild and free.
If it weren't for these walls and little steel door,
I'd be on my way, forgetting the days of yore.
But the sound I hear when the metal doors roll,
remind me for whom these hallowed bells toll.
I hear their message and I stay strong,
gazing out the window the horizon's long.
The night has come, in my bed I climb,
time to put an end, to this solemn rhyme.

So, for now I'll wait, and just bide my time,
for a fleeting glimpse, of the eternal sunshine.

64

Mother, 2002

I remember when I first heard you,
as I dwelt within the womb,
you said you'd love me forever,
no matter what I do.

You nurtured me with loving care,
as you carried me below,
and kept me safe inside you,
praying for me to grow.

There were few things that I knew,
in the darkness where I dwelt,
it was your voice I surely heard
and your love I always felt.

I listened to your voice,
as you sang to me in tune,
you whispered to me softly,
and said you'd see me soon.

It was here in the silence,
that I became real,
you fashioned me in your image,
using true love's will.

On the day that I was born,
when I first saw your face,
the love I felt from you,
I knew nothing could replace.

Father, 2002

I remember the first time,
you spoke to me in the womb,
you promised to always love me
regardless of the life I chose.

You spoke to me of promises,
described all the places we'd see,
all the things we'd do together
on all the journeys you'd take me.

Sometimes I felt you near me,
others, you seemed far away,
but I knew even then,
you thought of me every day.

Sometimes I felt your touch,
just beyond my reach,
beyond the walls around me,
soothing me to sleep.

It was here in the darkness
that I began to bloom,
fashioned in your likeness,
by a blending of love that's true.

On the day that I came forth,
I was quick to recognize,
the place I would always hold,
in my father's...loving eyes.

Posthumously, 2006

The feelings in the air listen to its ken,
and try to understand this pain that I am in.

You'll never really know the emptiness I see,
the loneliness that feeds this desire within me.

Will you even care, will you even cry,
when I leave this world and heaven far behind.

What will you think about someone you've known,
will you get the message from the patience I've shown.

You'll wonder how it was, ponder what it meant,
what I really felt when the moment came and went.

Just know that I was strong, I chose the way I left,
feeling only sweet relief as silence stole my breath.

Seasons of Rain, 1999

A cold wind blows its aura remains,
floatin' in the aether like a shroud of flame.
The sky will cry when seasons change,
cloudin' up the weather with snow and rain.

In Winter's heart the firmament's gray,
draped in a shroud it blankets the day.
A curtain of white swaddles the ground,
it's mother nature's way of spreading her gown.

Times do change, seasons do fade,
I know the rhyme and rhythm of rain.
Times will fade, the age will change,
life is the reason to enjoy each day.

Seasons die, the eras will fade,
can you tell me who makes the rain?
The milieu changes, Spring comes through,
sproutin' motley flowers in all colors and hues.

Amber grains roll on the Lea,
like giant waves on a golden sea,
A peaceful knoll upon the glen,
where shades of the Sun are shining again.

Upon the breeze, rides the coming rain,
I guess it's time, for the seasons to change,
Springtime shade, Autumn made,
all the leaves to color the rain.

Winter's heart, Summer's flame,
how can I capture the joys of rain,

Times change, the days will fade,
won't you tell me who makes the rain?

A zephyr blows, an arid wind,
warmin' the weather to herald Summer in.
A passionate hymn, season's paean,
Serenadin' the ether with thunder and rain.

Twilight shines on a dawn that's new,
painting the sky with a rainbow hue.
Sunshine brings, beautiful rays,
imbuing the wind, warmin' the day.

Weeks will fade, months will gray,
a warning sign to temper the way.
Days roll on, years will pass,
for purple mounts, and April's 'cast.

Seasons change, to shades of gray,
I will remember the song of rain.
The seasons turn, maelstroms glow,
with amber yellows, orange reds and gold.

Autumn brings, leaves that fall,
in a honey rain that festoons all.
A winsome bouquet bathes the air,
changing the flavor in the atmosphere.

A pattern weaves and flowers breed,
in pools of radiance under the trees.
Autumn's shade, Winter made,
all the snowflakes of December's mane.

Spring's heart, summer's flame,
I will remember the seasons of rain.

As It Be, 2003

Within the abyss from whence all came,
dwelt an essence without form,
drifting amidst the swirling chaos,
was a presence within the storm.

Dormant thoughts began to churn
coalescing among the vapor,
where its essence began to roam
and consciousness began to venture.

It journeyed beneath the empty twilight,
casting shadows near and far,
on an odyssey through the cosmos,
molding worlds among the stars.

Peering through the mists of creation
gazing down upon a tender world,
at the sea and storms that raged,
and the turmoil that unfurled.

Moving through the dark abyss,
across the visage of the deep,
fashioning life in its image,
from the dust beneath its feet.

Thus, life began among the world,
in the air, the water, and land,
where mankind would forever rule,
beneath the creator's hand.

Therein from man, a piece was taken
to bless him, with a woman so kind,
to join together in this life
in heart, soul, and mind.

A 16th of Grace, 2003

#1. May the Lord keep thine ears
deaf to the whispers
that attempt to bedevil thee
and lead thee astray.

#2. May the Lord shelter thee
from the evil
that walketh the Earth
in the guise of the righteous.

#3. May the Lord protect thee
from the shadows
that lie in wait,
intending to do thee harm.

#4. May the Lord grant thee
asylum from
the persecution
of thine enemies.

#5. May the Lord defend thee
against all foes
that may
revolt against thee.

#6. May the Lord shield thee
from
the weapons
of thine enemies.

#7. May the Lord champion thee
against evil
and
all its minions.

#8[2] May the Lord stand
betwixt thee and harm
in all
the dark places ye must travel.

#9. May the Lord preserve
thy soul, and the souls
of
thy kith and kin.

#10. May the Lord provide refuge
to thee
when though art amongst strangers,
and when thou art alone.

#11. May the Lord guard thee
when thou art at rest
upon
dusk and dawn.

#12. May the Lord's patience
endure when thou
becometh disheartened
and falter in thy faith.

#13. May the Lord's strength
sustain thee
in times of great turmoil
and despair.

#14. May the Lord's love
abide in
thy heart and mind,
for all eternity.

#15. May the Lord's blessings
dwell in
thine soul
perpetually.

#16. May the Lord's grace
forever bless thee
and find
favor in all the works ye do.

The Immortal Pen, 2011

Within the pen dwells the spirit
of all things we've yet to reveal,
it summons the essence of mind
to express the passion we feel.

The pen is tool of incomparable truth
one that bleeds with immortal fire,
the ink that flows from its nib
indites with the flame of desire.

There's a requisite silence in its stroke,
a humble peace in its glide,
it grants us license if we but listen
to the silent beauty inside.

Upon the page we bare our thoughts
and fashion them into gems,
where every line reveals the passion
of the soul that lies within.

Wistful Things 2015

Beneath the soil lay fertile seed
where wildflowers await the spring,
their buried hearts will soon be free
once they wake from gifted dream.

As burgeoning buds plenish the fields
and weave their charms of affection,
its subtle enchantment draws us close
and fills the heart with life's reflection.

'Tis the wind oft makes them sway
like courtiers among the lea,
dancing as though they were lovers
to the song of morning's breeze.

Descendant, 2012

Before me, palms upturned, a cradle appears,
it fills completely with morning lux,
and like a warm elixir it floods the chalice
branding my flesh one of its own.

Drawing close the cupped quiddity
I aspired dimensionally deep,
my progenitor's essence imbues me,
nurturing my being with immortal glory.

What I am feels its pith, pouring forth,
hemorrhaging from the astral verse,
it fills me with eternal residue
its copious hue stains my mind

Here, I am made manifest,
an epic disciple from the great abyss,
one spawned of celestial fires
forever named... scion of the stars.

The Specter of Worth Ship, 2001

Oh, Seraph of quietus, ye harvester of the bone bag,
harken unto me and spare thine precious counsel.
Hither, beneath thy wings, I beseech thee,
bear me to thy somatic garden,
and brand my wistful soul with thine immortal kiss.
Long have I pinned for such eternal repose,
yet I am routinely denied admittance to thine ossuary.

Oh, Culler of vice and virtue,
glimpsed have I your naked fangs,
covet do I those ivory razors,
and bid them draw forth the tepid claret
from this aging cask that is my mortal coil.

Tell me, oh Lord of Necropolis,
should I feel disgrace for want of
death's brush drawn across my canvas?
Should it truly be a bane to plead for such sweet release,
a return to my primordial essence?
Nay, from inception, this tenement of clay
was promised back to thine fold.

Come now, oh Master of Sleep,
none should suffer the indignity of
compulsory reproach for such fancy.
Neither hubris, nor impetuosity could
craft so eloquent a passion,

only the skein of providence permits one
to take leave of its salient gift.

If this be verily so, how then could such
a fervent prayer for my own euthanasia,
become an onus of shame I should bear?
Why then cannot the orison of my tormented heart,
become the saving grace of such a lamentable existence,
or be the final liberation from this
sardonic Sisyphean drama?

Pray tell, oh Titan of the Bone Dale,
hath not the iniquity of my life curried
such winsome favor in thine eye?
Must I continually prove my lack of
reticence to be wrapped in thy shroud,
to journey no more upon this primrose path?

I say to thee, oh Denizen of the Night,
begrudge not this vassal your sculptor's glaive.
Come forth, I implore thee and end this baleful
nightmare with thy steely embrace,
if I am found worthy...

...

...

...

Hello?

*

*

*

Author Bio

T.C. Monk is an eccentric soul, one of those people you want to seek out if you are looking for more than what's on the surface. Static of your own existence. His thoughts and views on the essence of life and its interconnectivity are not new, but the colorful manner in which he presents them in his writings is! All his talents are self-taught, not innate gifts he was born with.

He honed these skills during his lengthy incarceration and believes that coming to prison not only saved his life but also proffered him the opportunity to create something out of a broken life. His prior life in the free world was not exceptional. It fell short of what his mind needed: excitement, danger, the thrill of the chase, something that would push the threshold of propriety.

Being in prison did not teach him anything of value, as the system is not designed for teaching but rather for simply warehousing human beings. The time he was saddled with for his crimes allowed him to either use it to create something out of a nothing life or merely continue as others in prison do, letting themselves waste away and never leaving their mark on the world.

He has spent all his time in prison studying poetry, prose, ink and pencil art, history, language, philosophy, psychology, theology, and family and personal relationships. Courtesy, honesty, fidelity, trust, respect, honor, patience, and sacrifice are all traits he has fought to instill in himself in hopes of not only making something out of a wasted life but also proving that with dedication, discipline, and determination, anyone can change their life for the better. All they need do is try!

His wish is to give back a little of the grace the world saw fit to bestow upon a broken soul. He once was lost, but now he's found. Direct messaging with the author is available via email at www.securustech.net[1] (inmate name and ID #) or by snail mail to the Arizona Department of Corrections, Rehabilitation and Reentry, Timothy C. Monk, ADCRR #068675, Eyman Complex/Browning Unit, P.O. Box 211309, Dallas, Texas 75211.

---

[1] The first line of this poem as well as the last four words of the poem are taken from the movie, 'The Shape of Water.'

[2] Paraphrasing an old Egyptian blessing.

---

1. http://www.securustech.net

Don't miss out!

Visit the website below and you can sign up to receive emails whenever T.C. Monk publishes a new book. There's no charge and no obligation.

https://books2read.com/r/B-A-TGZAB-AROID

BOOKS2READ

Connecting independent readers to independent writers.

Did you love *Imperfections of Beauty*? Then you should read *Beautiful Imperfections*[2] by T.C. Monk!

[3]

'Beautiful Imperfections' is another gem of immeasurable brilliance within an ever-growing collection of illustrious jewels. This book is not a revision of the author's first book, *Imperfections of Beauty* (2022), but rather an expansive accumulation of thought and creativity that elevates his artistry to a new level of mastery. Within this volume is an ecumenical manual of creative vision, abundant charm, and timeless reflection, woven with care, insight, and wisdom. Alongside these varied sentiments are themes of insouciant cruelty,

2. https://books2read.com/u/38Ok2O

3. https://books2read.com/u/38Ok2O

profound pain, and unparalleled truth—elements that not only reveal the shadows of human frailty but also illuminate the enduring light of resilience.

www.ingramcontent.com/pod-product-compliance
Lightning Source LLC
Chambersburg PA
CBHW061336140726
47997CB00003B/1003